How To Recover From Pet Loss

Supporting You On Your Journey To Acceptance

By Wendy Andrew

How To Recover From Pet Loss

Copyright © 2020 by Wendy Andrew

All rights reserved.
No part of this book may be used or reproduced in any manner whatsoever without written permission except in the case of brief quotations embodied in critical articles or reviews. Permission was sought and granted by Julie Leonard, Dr Emee Vida Estacio, my friends and family members to be mentioned in this book.

For permissions contact: hello@counsellor.com

Edited by Michelle Martin

Disclaimer

This book is designed to provide information and motivation to our readers. While all attempts have been made to verify the information provided in this publication, neither the Author, nor the Publisher, assumes any responsibility for errors, omissions, or contrary interpretations on the subject matter herein. Any perceived slight of any individual or organisation is purely unintentional. The book is sold with the understanding that neither the Author nor the Publisher is engaged to render any type of psychological, medical, legal or any other kind of professional advice. Neither the Author nor the Publisher shall be held liable or responsible to any person or entity with respect to any physical, psychological, emotional, financial or commercial damages, including but not limited to, special, incidental, consequential or other damages or alleged to have been caused, directly or indirectly, by the information or programs contained herein. Every person is different, and the advice and strategies contained herein may not be suitable for your situation. Our views and rights are the same. **You are responsible for your own choices, actions, and results.**

Contents

PREFACE

DEDICATION

CHAPTER 1
- Anticipatory Grief 1

CHAPTER 2
- Denial 11

CHAPTER 3
- Anger 17

CHAPTER 4
- Bargaining 23

CHAPTER 5
- Guilt 26

CHAPTER 6
- Depression 33

CHAPTER 7
- Acceptance 39

CHAPTER 8
- How to Support Your Child 45

CHAPTER 9
- How to Support Others 51

CHAPTER 10
- Coping Mechanisms 58

REFERENCES 75

AUTHOR BIO 76

Preface

Dear Reader,

Firstly, I am so sorry for your loss. I would never presume to know how you are feeling but, having been through this experience several times myself, I know how utterly devastated and lost I felt. It is absolutely horrible but unfortunately as pet parents, unless you have a tortoise, you will already be aware that your pet will not live as long as you do. As harsh as this may sound, it's a sad fact of life and its o.k. to be upset despite having that knowledge. I like to think that we live longer so that we can love and care for more of them in our lifetime.

Secondly, I am writing this book for you. The 5 stages of Grief were introduced to the world by a psychiatrist named Elisabeth Kubler-Ross. The Kubler-Ross Model is also known by the acronym DABDA which stands for Denial, Anger, Bargaining, Depression and Acceptance and was originally intended support terminally ill patients come to terms with their situation however has come to be recognised in the context of grief and loss in any form. However, through my own experience, both personally and professionally, I know that there is also Anticipatory Grief and Guilt. Each emotion will be explored in its own dedicated chapter in addition to tips on how to support your child and others (in case you are not the grieving pet parent), suggestions for memorialising your pet and helpful coping strategies. You may experience some of these emotions or you may experience all of these emotions. Everyone has their own unique experience and there is no right or wrong way to feel. This is not a guidebook for grief but merely a way to reach out and let you know what to expect and how best to cope with whatever emotions you might be feeling.

Thirdly, I am here to help and support you on your journey to acceptance. I am passionate about letting people know that support is available for those who want or need it. Counselling is not for everyone but if I can help just one person at such a difficult time to feel better, recover quicker or provide some comfort then this was a book worth writing.

I am on a mission to combat Disenfranchised

Grief on your behalf and will always be an advocate for this. Disenfranchised Grief is grief which is not acknowledged or accepted by society. More often than not, this will come from those in your circle who have never had a companion animal however there can sometimes be a lack of support from those who just don't understand what you are going through or feel that the right to grieve is based on particular species. For me, it is a matter of respecting a person's feelings. You are perfectly entitled to feel whatever you are feeling, and nobody has the right to invalidate your feelings.

Much of this will be repeated and expanded upon throughout the book as I know that not everyone reads the preface and some people will jump straight to the chapters that are most relevant to them. I completely understand the eagerness to get answers and I am not offended in the least if anyone skips ahead. I would just like to emphasise that you will not fully heal from this traumatic experience unless you allow yourself to feel what you are feeling. There is no quick fix or magic formula and you cannot skip ahead straight into the coping mechanisms expecting to feel better if you do X, Y or Z. It doesn't work like that. Believe me, I've tried! But remember, you are not alone on this journey, I'm with you all the way and hopefully this book will give you an insight on how to identify, acknowledge and process your emotions so that you safely reach your destination of Acceptance.

Best wishes & Kindest regards,

Wendy x

Dedication

I would like to dedicate this book to my amaaazing friend Julie who is THE most awesome Life Coach (www.julieleonardcoaching.com) and her beloved cat Angel who is sadly no longer with us. Julie supported me through some enormous life changes and inspired me to write this book. Julie works internationally but lives in Munich, Germany where Angel spent his senior years. His passing during Lockdown 2020, unfortunately meant I was unable to support Julie and her family in person, which made me realise that I could reach out and help people I cannot counsel by writing a book. Without Julie & Angel there would be no book.

Thank you!

Chapter 1

Anticipatory Grief

Anticipatory Grief – *Refers to a feeling of grief occurring before an impending loss.*

It will come as a surprise to many people that we can start the grieving process some time in advance of the event, be it rehoming, euthanasia, as our pet ages or their health deteriorates. Feelings of loss, dread and guilt are common in this initial stage. It's almost like a crash course in grief where it hits you all at once and you worry and ruminate over something that has not yet happened.

If our pet has been given a terminal diagnosis by their vet, it is not uncommon to experience shock, panic and denial. We might question the diagnosis in the futile hope that there has been a mistake. We may not fully absorb the information being given to us during this conversation as we begin to panic and experience increased feelings of anxiety. We might also dwell on the cause of the illness and wonder if there was any way it could have been prevented or if we should have done something differently. We might try to bargain in a bid to prevent the inevitable happening. This cycle of negative thinking can seem never-ending as we research the condition, the treatment and/or pain relief options and the associated time scales. This can be extremely overwhelming as we begin to accept the news that we are given but rest assured this is a perfectly natural response under the circumstances. It all just seems like too much all at the one time and it is difficult to cope.

When we become aware that death is on the horizon, it is quite normal to consider when would be the right time to make that final appointment with the vet. We may conduct quality of life assessments, hyper-vigilantly looking for signs of distress and deterioration in order to do what is best for our beloved companion. Pet Md have a good Quality of Life Scale on their website based on work by Dr Alice

Villalobos which might be a useful tool to use. This is a good indicator for any species of companion animal. Dr Villalobos named it the HHHHHMM Scale which stands for Hurt, Hunger, Hydration, Hygiene, Happiness, Mobility and More good days than bad. Let's explore quality of life and what we should consider and be looking out for.

My personal recommendation is to have a specific calendar for your pet and to make a list of what your pet enjoys eating and doing. Over a set period of time, monitor their level of interest in play, exercise, food and their general demeanour. Observe their behaviour. Are they still engaging with you or hiding? Are they sleeping more than usual? Do they appear to be in pain or panting while resting? Are they still in control of their bowel/bladder? Are they losing weight? Are they still grooming themselves? Are they less mobile? Perhaps most importantly, has their condition improved, worsened or stayed the same? Marking on the calendar what is a good day and what is a bad day is not an exact science, but it is a useful visual aide to help you gather information to discuss with your vet. When the bad days significantly outnumber the good days, it is time to give that matter serious consideration.

Many of the markers, however, can be managed, such as mobility. There are several options available depending on the reason for a deterioration in mobility. Some time ago while I was out walking some client dogs in a local park, I saw an elderly golden retriever being towed in a wagon behind a bicycle by her owner. I remarked how wholesome this was to see, to which the owner said that although she (the dog) was not as mobile as she once was, she still liked to get out and about to enjoy the park. It was truly one of the sweetest and purest things I have ever seen. Not to mention a great example of pet parenting! My heart just about melted.

Pain can also be managed to a degree but when you feel that the pain relief is no longer working it may be time to reassess the situation. It can be extremely tough to watch our beloved companion animals deteriorating and suffering but at some point, we have to ask ourselves who we are keeping them going for…

One of the most painful aspects of pet

bereavement (in my opinion) is guilt. At this point, guilt goes hand in hand with rumination. It is very easy to spend hours at a time thinking about causes of illness or disease. We often beat ourselves up mercilessly for not noticing symptoms of ill health earlier or wondering if we were in some way responsible. Should we have fed them differently or exercised them more? Even in the case of old age we can torment ourselves over whether or not it's the right time. Are we are acting too soon or indeed should we be acting sooner? We can often wonder if there might be an improvement in our pet's condition and ask ourselves if we should hold off. That is then countered by wondering if we are perhaps being selfish and prolonging our pet's discomfort if we wait. The quality of life assessment is also applicable here. We are perhaps not ready to say our last goodbyes to our beloved companion which is heartbreakingly understandable. But realistically, what good will come of asking ourselves so many questions? Would this change the outcome? Logically we know that the answer is that the outcome would not be different, but it is very difficult to apply logic during such an emotionally distressing time.

In cases of rehoming, guilt can be just as prevalent. We might wonder about our pet's future happiness and wellbeing or wonder if they will be as loved by their new care givers. We might wonder if there is still time to figure out an alternative. We might worry about a new relationship where our partner is highly allergic and wonder if it is a relationship that will last or fail. Being a bit of an overthinker myself, I might be inclined to wonder if it is a sign that this is not the right partner for me! We might ask ourselves if we really need or want to take that job opportunity abroad or that promotion that has working hours that would be incompatible with having a pet. The work/life balance is after all increasingly coming into focus and with so many health benefits to pet ownership, this is a valid point to consider. I myself had a job at one point where I worked a varied shift pattern. This meant it would have been unfair to have a dog (always my pet of choice!) as I would be out of the house for extended periods of time and that didn't sit well with me even with the option of a dog walker. Dogs like company so I can perfectly understand the dilemma this would pose to many people.

Due to this heightened emotional state, it is also quite common to experience sleep disruption. With all these thoughts and questions running through our minds it is, in a way, almost to be expected as we try to come to terms with what is going on. Even though it is emotionally draining and exhausting, it can still be very difficult to sleep, thus it becomes a vicious circle. I practice meditation with many of my clients to combat this constant mind chatter and although meditation is an incredibly beneficial way to start the day, it is also a greatly beneficial way to end it. As you lie in bed, the best way to achieve sleep naturally is to enter a relaxed state with a quiet mind. We will examine this in more detail in a later chapter which explores healthy coping strategies.

I mentioned earlier that 'Anticipatory Grief' can be surprising but what is perhaps even more surprising than the occurrence of anticipatory grief is that it can actually be beneficial in preparing you for the time ahead. It also gives you the opportunity to make the most of what time is left and to make special memories. This is the case for both rehoming and end of life situations. During this time, you could take a special trip or spend extra time appreciating a favourite walk. This is a great opportunity to take lots of nice photographs for a memory box or a dedicated photo album. You could make special meals for your pet (although perhaps in cases of deteriorating health, it is best to check with your vet first in case of tummy upsets). Even just simply spending more cuddle time and giving extra attention can be very comforting as sometimes we take time for granted and fail to make the most of it. We come to appreciate these precious moments of unconditional and reciprocated love more as we learn that we do not have as much time as we once thought we did and reprioritise. Sometimes even wishing we had reprioritised earlier and not spent so much time doing meaningless things. It is a good time to evaluate and reflect. Being present and in the moment becomes increasingly important.

In the event of euthanasia, it is good practice to have a conversation with your vet regarding the final appointment itself and what to expect. It is a very personal decision as to whether the euthanasia will occur at home or at the veterinary practice. It is also a personal decision whether to be present or not. My personal preference is to be there to hold and comfort my pet in their final moments before they go. I could not stand the thought of them wondering where I went and why I left them. But, as I say, I am an over thinker. If, however, you feel it would be too upsetting to be present, take comfort knowing that they would be treated with kindness, care and compassion by the vet staff. Some people prefer to be left with a living memory and that's ok too. It can be a very upsetting experience however it is also upsetting to regret something you may wish you had done differently later. So please give this a great deal of consideration. There is no do-over.

The word 'Euthanasia' comes from the Greek language meaning 'Good Death'. I will tell you something of what to expect as not everybody does. Most passings are peaceful however, some are not. It is possible to have your pet sedated prior to euthanasia if they are already showing signs of distress or anxiety to make it less stressful. Around 10-15 minutes later, the life ending drugs, also known as a barbiturate (usually pentobarbital), will be administered causing unconsciousness as the brain shuts down followed by respiratory or cardiac arrest. We would expect the evacuation of bodily fluids but sometimes there can also be spasms and involuntary body movements, sometimes even what appears to be a gasp for breath. This can be distressing to see however I feel it is only fair to offer transparency on this so that you can prepare yourself and make an informed decision on how to proceed. But please know that your pet will be completely unaware of these involuntary reactions and they are not the norm. Most importantly, they will not be in pain.

Chapter 2

Denial

Denial – *An assertion that something said, believed, alleged, etc., is false.*

Essentially denial is a defence mechanism which is activated to protect us from something that we are not ready to accept. It slows everything down. The thought of it could be too overwhelming and we feel that we just cannot cope with this information right now or that it may take a while to process. Part of this feeling of disbelief can come from the sheer shock of a sudden death. It can be very difficult to imagine life without our companion animal and we are not even close to being able to disconnect from them. It is much easier to put a block up and deny that this is happening. In a sense, this is not altogether a bad thing, as it acts a bit like a buffer. Our logical mind knows what has happened but emotionally we are just not ready to accept it. And that is ok. It can take some time, and everyone gets there at their own pace. You might just need to take a minute but take care not to pitch camp and stay here for too long.

As a young girl, I had the most delightful Labrador called Honey. She was exactly that colour and just as sweet. I grew up on the very outskirts of Glasgow, in a lodge house which was built in 1856, surrounded by farmland and on the edge of a forest. This was absolutely perfect for all 3 of our Labradors to explore, but Honey was my responsibility and was an incredibly inquisitive girl who liked to go off on an adventure. I loved her beyond measure. She was my best friend, companion and teenage confidante. She was my first pet of my very own and that was incredibly special to me. I felt a great sense of responsibility and I was so proud that my parents felt I was ready to take on that responsibility and care for her myself. We would often go off on adventures through the forest together, me on my BMX and her running alongside me. As this was a 'safe' semi-rural

Denial

setting, and the mid-1980s, nobody really bothered about her adventures because all of the families living in the forest knew each other's dogs. Plus, being a Labrador and completely ruled by her stomach, she always returned home for her dinner. Usually covered in mud, as Labradors often do! However, one day she did not return, and we had a knock on our door that evening which was most unusual given our location. To my horror, it was a motorist with tears streaming down his face, telling us that he had hit Honey with his car... It was a moment that pains me even now, all these years later, to think of.

I could not believe this had happened. Surely not my Honey. It must have been another dog. I was so shocked. My parents went outside with the motorist who was understandably very upset. None of us blamed him for this terrible accident, but I just could not believe this was happening. My parents confirmed that she was still alive, although obviously very badly injured, and rushed her to the vet. It was set in my head that she would be fine despite the evidence to the contrary. Sadly, she did not make it through the night and succumbed to internal injuries.

I felt numb and utterly lost without my girl. I was in a complete daze until the next morning when we received the update from the vet. I was so hopeful that everything would be alright and that she would pull through despite being told that this was highly unlikely. She was young, fit and healthy so I was certain that she would survive. This hope slowed the process down for me because, although I knew it was unlikely to be a positive outcome, I needed that time to process everything that had happened and was still going on. I believe that the shock, denial and numbness gave me a degree of protection before having to accept that this tragic event had occurred.

Denial can, as previously mentioned, be part of anticipatory grief for very much the same reason. If we are told that our companion animal has a terminal illness, very often our first thought is that there must be a mistake. Even when logically we know there has not been a mistake and that we have sought medical attention after noticing symptoms. We just cannot allow ourselves to believe this to be true. Similarly, with an elderly companion animal, we may have known that they may not last too much longer. But

Denial

when it inevitably happens, we have to hit the pause button for a moment, and that's o.k. It is important to take that time out and process the information. It is o.k to ask as many questions as you want or need to in order to absorb and process the information being given. This is just how we give ourselves time to adjust to a new reality and accept what has happened.

Sometimes denial can manifest as not wanting to talk about it. We may not have the words to express ourselves yet or are maybe just not ready to talk about it. But failing to acknowledge it and actively avoiding the subject does no good in the long run. It also makes it difficult for others to support us. By shutting down or by shutting our loved ones out, they could mistakenly believe that we are fine and that no support is required or wanted. Hopefully those closest to us will observe a 'bottling up' scenario and wait it out until we are ready.

In the short term, denial is not problematic as such, however a prolonged period of denial can indeed be harmful and extends the grieving process quite considerably and prevents us from moving forward. It is extremely easy to get stuck in this stage as we do not consciously *want* to move past this stage and accept that what is happening is real. We might even deny that we are in denial so that people stop bothering us about our denial. As uncomfortable, cruel and painful as the reality is, we must move forward and acknowledge that our companion is no longer with us. Coming out of denial is a huge, brave and positive step forward as we begin to accept what has happened. It just became real and we can begin to process the information.

Chapter 3

Anger

Anger – *A strong feeling of displeasure and belligerence aroused by a wrong.*

Anger can very often erupt from frustration that we have absolutely no control over what has happened. Our lives have changed forever with the loss of our companion animal and there is absolutely nothing that we can do about it. This situation, particularly with death, is completely outwith our control and for many of us, this is a completely alien concept. Most of us would like to believe that we, pretty much, are the captains of our own ships and that we are in control of our lives. As pet parents, we have control over every aspect of our pet's lives. We make all the decisions for them. Although, I am sure there are a few notable exceptions which may invoke fond memories of times when they completely disobeyed us in favour of doing their own thing. I will never tire of hearing such stories if you ever want to share them with me on my social media platforms or during counselling sessions.

In cases of accidental death, it is quite instinctive to feel anger towards the person we perceive to be responsible for the accident. Someone may have run over our cat or, in my case, dog. Someone may have left a window open and let our birds escape. Someone may have set off a firework which spooked our pet and they took off which may result in a terrible accident occurring or in some cases have even died of a heart attack/fright because of it. Silent fireworks do exist. In my humble opinion, all fireworks should be silent for the sake of the animals/wildlife and indeed veterans with ptsd, but that's another battle for another day. Someone may have even stolen our pet and in that case, we would have every right to feel extremely angry. We might even be angry at ourselves for those very same reasons as we may hold ourselves responsible. I know that I certainly felt extremely angry with myself for assuming that Honey would

Anger

return home as normal and even more so that I did not go looking for her. I felt angry at myself for not preventing the terrible accident which ultimately resulted in her death. However, accidents, by definition, are unintentional and we must try to remember that during this difficult time. It is highly unlikely that anyone would intentionally hit our pet with their car or leave an escape route open for them. But, by the same token, rational and logical thinking can often be lacking during the grieving process.

I am not a particularly religious person, but I know that sometimes those in the midst of grief can be angry at God or whichever deity they believe in. In most instances of pet loss, it is almost a certainty that we will ask why this has happened to our companion or ask, 'Why me?'. We will look to the powers that be for answers and ask how they could allow this awful thing to happen. Sadly, sometimes we have to accept that there is no reason or explanation to be had and that in itself is hugely frustrating when we are desperate to make sense of things and find comfort in the answers we are looking for.

We can be angry at an ex-partner who has

refused to let us take custody of our joint pet or perhaps angry that they will not let us see them. It can cause great anger to feel like the rug has been pulled from under our feet. Unfortunately, pets are often 'collateral damage' when it comes to a separation or break-up. No matter how hard this may be to accept on a personal level, if we take a more compassionate view, it becomes a little more understandable why they may have reached that decision. We might have failed to acknowledge that our ex-partner is grieving the loss of the relationship and does not feel able to cope with maintaining that link. They may also be in a better position to the primary caregiver to the pet for various reasons.

If we have to rehome our pet, that can also cause a great deal of anger and frustration. We may feel anger towards a new landlord who does not permit pets or anger towards our employer who is forcing a relocation or longer working hours. There may be a little wiggle room under these circumstances if the landlord or employer is a 'pet person' themselves. There is generally a lack of understanding which breeds contempt towards those making or influencing decisions and big life changes on our behalf and towards those who just do not understand the pain of pet loss. It can be incredibly frustrating when circumstances are outwith our control.

The most well-meaning of friends and family members can also be recipients of our wrath. On many occasions throughout our lives we lash out in anger and hurt those closest to us. Even when they are trying to be helpful. They may just have said the wrong thing at the wrong time. Anger is a strong emotional response to the feeling of hurt and pain. We must however be mindful that the emotion of anger does not escalate to acts of aggression or violence as our ability to self-regulate diminishes (as does judgement). Again, if we try to view things from a different perspective, we may see things differently. Even if it is irritatingly well intended.

Anger can be quite a destructive emotion and have a negative impact on our own health and wellbeing according to several university research papers. Symptoms such as headaches, increased blood pressure, insomnia and even IBS (Irritable Bowel Syndrome). The body produces more stress hormones such as adrenaline and cortisol. As our heart rate, blood pressure and respiration increase, we can feel increasingly anxious as well as angry. If we already have health issues relating to the heart and blood pressure, this can be particularly dangerous. Anger also puts us at an increased risk of strokes. According to a study by Harvard University, anger can decrease levels of immunoglobulin A thus having a negative effect on our immune system which in turn leaves us less able to fight off infections and illnesses.

In addition to the physical aspect, our minds can become very preoccupied with this emotion causing a lack of concentration which can be dangerous if we are not paying full attention to everyday tasks, whilst driving for example, making the possibility of accidents more likely. It is completely understandable how this distracting and all-consuming emotion can cause us to lose focus but if we are aware of this then we are in a better position to do something about it.

If you feel that your anger is prolonged, escalating, disproportionate, misdirected or unmanageable then I strongly recommend seeking professional help.

Chapter 4

Bargaining

Bargaining – *An agreement between parties settling what each shall give and take or perform and receive in a transaction.*

It is normal to make a desperate attempt to avoid grief by mentally bargaining and perhaps 'making a deal with God' or whichever deity we believe in. If they can stop or change 'this' then we will never complain about 'that' again. We will never complain about getting woken up at silly o'clock for peepees ever again. We will never complain about scratched furniture or shredded curtains ever again. We will never complain about mucking out a stable on a cold winter day ever again. We will never complain about constant and slightly annoying early morning chirping ever again. These feelings of despair and anxiety leave us frantically searching for somewhere to turn to as we cannot accept that what we are experiencing is really happening. We have that last grain of hope that there is still a way back from this and we can fight against what we know to be true.

This hope is false hope and sadly this process of negotiation is futile. At this stage we can often feel very vulnerable and helpless therefore this can be seen as an attempt to regain control of the situation. We hope we can perhaps have an opportunity to do things differently to avoid the outcome. Or perhaps to delay the inevitable and gain a little more time in the hope of a medical breakthrough or that a miracle cure can be found. In cases of old age, it's quite common to bargain for more time with our beloved companion as we're just not emotionally ready to let go. It is another demonstration of self-preservation in this process, much like denial. It gives us a moment to take a break from the pain and anguish that we are feeling. Our emotions are put on hold for a moment while we try to strike this deal that will change everything. We feel hopeful again that things will go back to normal and that we can stay in our comfort zone. Except that, in reality, we know that nothing will change and there is no deal to be had.

When Honey died, I know that I made all kinds of promises including never letting her off the lead ever again and never complaining about chewed shoes. Sadly, my silent and tearful pleas fell on deaf ears. I realised that I couldn't negotiate my way out of this and had to accept that this was real, and this was happening. That made me incredibly sad.

This desperation can be very tough for those around us to watch. But the 'good' thing about this stage, if we can say there is anything good about it, is that it usually does not last too long if it's experienced at all. Which is why this is such a short chapter.

Chapter 5

Guilt

Guilt – *A feeling of responsibility or remorse for some offense, crime, wrong, etc., whether real or imagined.*

Guilt and Anger very often go hand in hand. It is that internalised anger that evolves into guilt. More often than not, the internal conflict of not doing or seeing something we think we should have and feeling like we neglected our duties as a pet parent in some way. Logically this is seldom the case but, as previously stated, logic rarely applies at this time. Guilt is by far the most common emotion I see displayed in my clients and what they struggle with the most.

I have had clients who activated very well organised search parties and go looking for their missing pets, post online and offer rewards for information. Some people are lucky and are reunited with their beloved pets, but some people are not. Whether you take action or not, nobody can predict what the outcome will be which causes frustration, anger and guilt because the outcome was not in our control.

Once I got over the initial shock of Honey being run over, I was utterly wracked with guilt. I was very experienced with dogs and should have done better. Dogs had been part of the family longer than I had so I should have been more careful. I should not have been complacent. Why did I assume she would come home and not go looking for her?... The reason I assumed she would come home is because she always did. Being a Labrador, she was a greedy girl and always came home for her dinner. I had no reason to think that that this would ever not be the case. A 33 acre forest is an amazing place for a dog to go sniffing around, gathering information and gaining mental nourishment from a good 'scent walk'. I may not have found her in time had I gone looking for her anyway as that is a big area to cover even for the whole family. We lived pretty much in the country and there was no reason to think she would be hit by a car. A tragic accident happened. However, the silver lining that I can now see is that I learned from this experience.

My current companion is a Pomchi (Pomeranian x Chihuahua) called Pixie and boy does she suit her name! The mischievous little elf that she is! A bit of a change from a Labrador but I would not change her for the world. She might be small, but she has a big personality and an abundance of character. We currently live in an urban environment with more than a few cars around. I adopted Pixie when she was two years old and it is the best thing I ever did. She brings me so much joy. However, she does enjoy a good bark and likes to chase people up the street. Particularly school children. I can appreciate that she thinks that she is just doing her job and chasing potential intruders away from our home. However, after what happened to Honey, I felt it was best to put up a gate and block all possible escape routes from the garden with chicken wire. I now feel that I have done everything possible to prevent her from being knocked down in the street by a vehicle. Princess Pixie Powderpuff, to give her her full name, is far too precious to me to take any risks. I am aware that I'm quite obsessive about the gate being closed at all times but I'm ok with that. I have my reasons. I think it is important that we don't beat ourselves up too much and see it as a lesson learned. If we learn from our mistakes and change our behaviour, then the outcome should be different should we find ourselves in a similar situation in the future.

I have also had clients who have experienced terrible feelings of guilt because they did not take their pet to the vet sooner to seek a diagnosis for an ailment. Without being a vet themselves, how could they possibly know? A lump could just be fatty tissue (lipoma) or a cyst. Laboured breathing could be allergies and in cases of brachycephalic breeds of dogs, such as boxers, pugs and bull dogs, this can be very difficult to spot as, due to their short muzzles and flat faces, they can often sound a bit laboured on a hot day anyway. There are so many things that we berate ourselves for that we could not have done any differently or had any knowledge of.

Another source of guilt is knowing when it is the right time to take our companion animals to the vet for the final time. As discussed in chapter 1, this is often part of anticipatory guilt in addition to after the event. My mother suffered terrible guilt, feeling that she had waited too long with our other 2 Labradors, Sam and Gemma. Gemma was very elderly, and her general health and mobility were deteriorating. Sam was epileptic and his seizures were becoming more frequent and severe. During a routine check-up, the vet discovered lumps which turned out to be cancerous. Euthanasia was the kindest thing to do for both of them after carrying out quality of life assessments however my mother was so in love with her dogs that she just wanted to have a bit more time. She experienced all the symptoms of anticipatory grief and then asked herself why she was keeping them going. She came to the conclusion that she had been verging on the side of selfishness and keeping them alive for herself despite their deteriorating health. At that point she made the heart-breaking decision to make that final appointment with the vet for them. To this day she wishes that she hadn't waited so long in case Sam and Gemma were suffering a moment longer than necessary.

I always tell my clients that euthanasia is the

ultimate act of compassion and kindness. It is a decision made from a place of love.

Not all feelings of guilt come from the death of a companion animal of course. There are many reasons why we may feel like the right thing to do is to rehome our pet. The main source of guilt under these circumstances comes from concern for their future wellbeing. We might worry that they are not as loved or well cared for by their new family. We might wonder if we really need to relocate or if there is a way we can figure out to keep our pet. But again, ultimately the decision-making process is the same. We do what is in the best interests of the animal. Would it be fair to have them left alone for long periods of time? Are we in a position to give them the care that they need? It is known to be beneficial to our physical, mental and emotional health to have a pet however, if any aspect of our health deteriorates to such a level that we are not able to provide care then it is most definitely time to consider what would be the right thing to do. A pet parent suffering addiction issues may be unable to care for their companion and may feel extreme guilt for not being able to get clean and sober. No pet parent would want their companion animal to receive anything less than the best care available and if that can not come from ourselves, for whatever reason, then we would be doing the right thing by them finding a place where they will be safe, well cared for and happy.

Guilt can also come from a simple momentary lapse in concentration. Particularly with horses, we might wonder if we left the gate open. Perhaps we closed it but then somebody else left it open afterwards. Sometimes we will just never know. So, would it really be logical to ruminate on questions we will never know the answer to? The logical answer to that is 'no, it would not be logical'.

The best advice I can give to anyone suffering in the guilt stage of grief is that they should always remember that they did the best they could with the information they had at the time. A great tool that I was reminded of by Dr Emee Vida Estacio, a professor of psychology, is the 'TLC' method. Is it true? Is it logical? Is it constructive? These are especially important questions to ask yourself when you are feeling guilty.

Chapter 6

Depression

Depression – *A condition of general emotional dejection and withdrawal; sadness greater and more prolonged than that warranted by any objective reason.*

Once we realise that bargaining does not work, it can be quite easy to fall into the clutches of depression as our feelings of hope fade. This in itself is a multi-faceted emotion. Indeed, it is a medical condition in its own right. Not everyone has the same experience of it and very often it can be difficult to see the light at the end of the tunnel.

At this point, I would like to share with you, that this was the toughest chapter in this book for me to write. It was difficult to even begin this chapter and I admit that I did a little bit of avoidance behaviour before getting stuck into it... I have anxiety and depression... I tell you this, not to seek sympathy or start a pity party, but to let you know that I can relate. I can also tell you, from personal experience, that there is indeed light at the end of the tunnel.

My anxiety and depression did not come from the loss of a pet but predominantly from a previous job and the people I encountered there. There were things going on in my life at that time which I was trying to find solutions for, in addition to my own physical and mental health issues, but I felt so unsupported, under pressure and that my employers were just ticking boxes and following procedure before I would inevitably lose my job due to my poor attendance record. I went through the emotions of feeling a lack of control, extreme sadness, feeling like a failure and completely useless. Some days I wanted to just scream and other days I could not find it within myself to get out of my bed. It all felt very hopeless and I was swinging between living in a fog and living in a state of despair. My perception was that people would view me as weak and a loser because of my depression but I am happy to tell you, my perception was completely wrong. With the support and guidance of my dear friend and life coach Julie Leonard, I found my tribe within the dog walking community when I started my own business. I found that others had had similar experiences. The general consensus was that depression is not a weakness, it's that you have tried to stay strong for too long.

Fast forward to the present day, the despair I once felt has vanished, I am a successful entrepreneur (although I dislike that word intensely), I retrained as a Pet Bereavement Counsellor and found my purpose in supporting others. Oh yeah, and now I'm an author! I have created a life that makes me very happy, but I wouldn't say that I no longer have anxiety and depression as I don't believe it ever really leaves you. I do have it under control, I have been unmedicated for several years and the time between bouts of it does get longer and longer to the point that I barely notice it's there anymore. The anxiety pops up from time to time, but I am now equipped to deal with it in my own way. Change is possible and you **can** create the life you once dreamed of. But it does help if you have a good support network of family and friends (and not forgetting my wonderful doctor). I was extremely fortunate in that respect and I do not take a single person for granted. Anything is possible when you let go of limiting beliefs and negative self-talk.

So, enough about me, back to the matter in hand. Of course, the base line of depression is extreme sadness and low mood however, generally speaking, it goes beyond this. Very often those suffering from depression will feel like they are slightly detached from reality. It's inconceivable that we will never see our beloved companion again and the loneliness that this realisation brings is almost unbearable. It's a horrible feeling and that is one of the reasons why I am so passionate about supporting people through the grieving process.

I can fully appreciate that feeling of not wanting to get out of bed. When we get out of bed, that's when the day officially starts, and we have to face reality. There is a moment when we first open our eyes when we feel happy and everything seems o.k. but then we remember what has happened and the world comes crashing down again. In this moment, we don't really want to face reality so staying in bed feels like the best option. Bed feels like a safe place to be. It can take some time before we feel like we might want to go out or see anyone. We can lose track of time altogether. It just doesn't seem very important. Nothing seems very important anymore. One notable symptom of depression can be that we neglect our self-care practices and personal hygiene as we just can't be bothered or face doing anything. Giving up on ourselves is an extremely easy thing to do but we mustn't. Please know that self-care is important because *you* are important. Self-care is more than just taking a bubble bath but it's not a bad place to start. We may not feel like cooking or eating but getting the right nutrition will give us what we need to feel better.

I do want you to be aware that other people may view this stage as a gross overreaction when it comes to pet bereavement. My message to you is, just ignore them, this is not their journey and they have no idea how you are feeling in this moment. Grief is a very personal thing, and everyone has a vastly different experience. Just because they didn't experience any depression, it doesn't mean that you are doing it wrong. It doesn't mean that they did it wrong either.

It's just different. You are not weak. You are grieving the loss of your best friend and it hurts. A lot.

In the depths of depression and despair, we might feel temporarily that life is too difficult, and we can't go on without our companion. If this is the case, I would strongly encourage you to make an appointment to see your doctor.

Chapter 7

Acceptance

Acceptance – *The act of assenting or believing.*

When the 'Good Days' outweigh the 'Bad Days' I think that is a decent indicator that we are approaching the stage of acceptance. The moments of peace we feel when we wake up will last a little longer. We might feel a bit more sociable as we accept the new reality that our companion animal is not there anymore. Of course, we are still incredibly sad about that, but we no longer deny that this is the case. We no longer cling on to the false hope that they will magically reappear when we open the front door. We can acknowledge that our beloved pet has died and that we will be ok. We might not actually be ok with it for a while, but we know that will come in the future and we have found the strength to talk about them without crying or shedding a tear at the thought of them. The pain and distress may be replaced by fondness and warmth in moments of reflection. It can feel like quite an emancipation to be free of the feelings of Denial, Anger, Bargaining, Guilt and Depression which are not as intense as they once were. As we move into a more positive state of mind, we can allow ourselves to let go of the negative feelings surrounding our loss. We can let go of the anger which had such a strong grip. We can let go of the guilt and stop blaming ourselves. We can let go of the depression we thought we would never survive… because we did! We did survive it!

It is a really tough and emotional journey to get to this stage in the grieving process so be kind to yourself and give yourself some credit. I'm certainly proud of every single person who reaches this stage whether I know them or not. It is a huge achievement to lose a loved one, experience all these emotions and accept this as the new normal.

A friend of mine who recently had her beloved Lurcher euthanised due to old age and ill health, took

Acceptance

the decision to rehome two adorable little Chihuahuas from a rescue centre as her home felt so empty without Axel. She was worried that this was being disrespectful to his memory or if he would not have been happy about it. I was keen to reassure her, having known the old chap for many years, he would have been very proud of her for providing a good and loving home to not one but two dogs who might otherwise not have been so fortunate to be given the same life that he had with her and her son. Of course, she still misses Axel terribly, but she is oh so in love with Chewie and Tia. That's a great comfort to me as her friend and I am ever so proud of her.

Another friend lost her cat to cancer of the mouth. She couldn't stand to see poor Jonesy in any degree of pain or suffering. So, after a few rounds of treatment the time came after discussing the best option with the vet and a quality of life assessment. The decision was made. After saying for several months that she wasn't ready for another cat… Rosie and Juliette, a couple of stunning Russian Blues, came by way of another friend. They needed a new home. Her friend had decided to progress his relationship and move his girlfriend into his home however she was highly allergic to the cats. Utterly distraught at what to do for the best, my friend decided that they would be best off with her and she gives them as much love as cats allow! Cosy Rosie, as she is commonly referred to, is quite happy to cuddle but Juliette is a bit more aloof.

One of the surest ways to determine that you have reached the stage of acceptance is when you feel like you might want to open your heart and home to another companion animal. Your past pets will never be replaced by new pets, but your heart may be open to that love again someday. Only you will know when you and indeed your family are ready. I know myself that my heart has felt empty or like there was a big Labrador shaped hole in it. But, if I may throw myself out there again as an example. That big Labrador shaped hole has been filled by a wonderful little Pomchi. I do not feel any guilt about moving on and loving another pet because I know in my heart that Honey would be proud of me for showing the same love and affection to Pixie by giving her a new forever home. She would be proud of me for learning from experience.

Throughout the writing of this book, I have had tears running down my face and smothered that little rascal with kisses as I didn't get to give Honey a final kiss and for the life of me, I can't recall when that last kiss was as it all happened so suddenly. Ergo, Pixie gets absolutely smothered with affection and spoiled rotten. No wonder she's such a Diva!

This is the stage where we might be ready to memorialise our pet in some way. There are many ways to do this if that is your wish. You would plant a tree in memory of your companion animal and perhaps use this place to scatter their ashes. You may decide instead to have a piece of jewellery made from their ashes. There are many businesses who can be found online who offer this service. I have recommended several local artists to commission paintings of pets in various styles from caricatures to oils and even a ceramic artist who makes the most amazing little models. One of my favourite suggestions to memorialise a deceased cat or dog is a to purchase a beautiful plant in a round pot which you can admire and nurture and place their collar around.

A kind gesture would also be to make a donation to an animal charity in your pet's name. There will be more suggestions on ways to memorialise your pet as a family in the next chapter.

Chapter 8

How to Support Your Child

Perhaps even more distressing that our own tears are the tears of a child. While we are grieving ourselves, it can be incredibly difficult to know how to support our children or indeed the children within our circle.

I would strongly reinforce that honesty is the best policy and be appropriate for the age of the child. Any attempts to shield a child from what is going on can result in them imagining the worst possible scenario or drawing their own conclusions which could lead to unnecessary anxiety. Sadly, death and separation are part of life and in the context of a companion animal, this could be a child's first experience of death or separation so it's important to get it right.

If you are rehoming a family pet, it may be a good idea to involve your child in the discussion and explain to them the circumstances which have made it impossible to keep the pet. By letting them know that all avenues have been explored and that this is the best option available for said pet, the child will be fully informed and find it easier to process.

In cases of euthanasia, again honesty is the best policy. Always refer to the death as a death. Do not refer to it as being 'put to sleep' as this again, can cause a great deal of anxiety for children. They may become afraid of sleep or worry about family members going to sleep and never waking up. Can open, worms everywhere so avoid, avoid, avoid. If your pet was seriously ill, explain to your child that they were seriously unwell and that their body couldn't fight the illness. If your pet was involved in an accident, explain that they were very badly injured, and they couldn't be fixed. I would recommend steering clear of saying that the vet couldn't fix them because this could cause the child to feel anger towards the vet. Anger is not a healthy emotion, particularly for children, and is difficult for them to process and self-regulate. If your pet is elderly, explain to your child that your pet was old and that their body wasn't working as well as it used to. You might even

How to Support Your Child

be able to explain that animals tend not to live as long as people do and that this is just a natural thing that happens. It's nobody's fault. If you lie to your child and they find you out, you will have broken their trust. I would also avoid bringing God into the picture by saying that your pet was so good that God wanted them by His side. This could absolutely scare the bejesus out of any child. Just don't go there. Again, I quite like to say that we live longer than they do so that we can give loving homes to more of them.

I was on a university placement in Cape Cod, Massachusetts, USA and I wasn't told until shortly before I was due to return to Scotland that Sam and Gemma were no longer with us. I don't share this to bash my family because with hindsight I know their intentions were good, but I was utterly devastated. The very last thing I said to Gemma whilst ruffling her big golden velvety ears was that I would see her in six months. I felt like I had let her down by not being there to say goodbye and that I had made a false promise. Sam, who was the most handsome black Labrador, got a good old butt scratch on my way out the door. I knew Gemma was very old, but I didn't know that Sam had cancer. I was abroad, alone, grieving and nobody had discussed it with me. The house felt so horribly empty without them when I arrived home and my heart just broke.

Always allow your child to grieve but reassure them that it was not their fault and that they have not been abandoned. It is especially important to give this reassurance if the companion animal ran away or escaped. It would be far easier to be honest and tell the child that the animal/bird perhaps got a fright and ran away and that sometimes when that happens they go into survival mode or that they may have gotten lost and can't find their way home. On the subject of 'running away', don't use this as an excuse or alternative for death. It will give a child false hope by saying that their pet has run away, and this may inspire the child to go looking for them or anticipate their return which prevents them from grieving and reaching acceptance.

It can be quite normal for a young child to have lots of questions and it is also quite common for their behaviour to take a turn for the worse. As previously mentioned, they don't have the same ability to self-regulate that adults do. This is just their way of processing so please be understanding, compassionate and remember that this is coming from a place of pain and upset. If you yourself are upset, do not hide your tears from your child. It's important that they know it's ok to cry. My father, to this day, refuses to have another dog despite our occasional requests in the hope that he might have changed his mind. He just can't go through the loss again which is completely understandable, and we all accept this.

Let your child know that you are there for them if they need a comforting hug, no matter how big they are, and that you are open to talking to them about their experience and willing to listen. If your child is a teenager they may not want to talk to you about how they are feeling so it may be an idea to ask for support from a friend or other family member with whom they have a good relationship.

There are several ways to memorialise a family pet. For younger children, it might be comforting for them to draw a picture or 50 of their pets as a way to express themselves. You could write a letter to your pet together which would help your child get their bottled-up feelings out and on to paper which would give you the opportunity to discuss how they are feeling. You could write a story about your pet together, perhaps about a great adventure which might provoke a happy memory for your child to treasure. There are companies who will illustrate and publish such books as a nice keepsake. Older children might prefer to write a poem. Other keepsakes such as collars, horseshoes and toys may be placed in a memory box or you may wish to create a special photo album for your pet together. Going through photographs together may also provide an opportunity for your child to talk about your pet and how they are feeling so I believe this is a worthwhile thing to do. If a tree has been planted in your pet's honour, your children may take comfort in making this event a memorial service where they get to speak about their pet in a cathartic way.

It may also be helpful to inform their teachers that your child is grieving for their pet so that they can be supportive and understanding of any upset or behaviour which may be out of character.

Chapter 9

How to Support Others

It can be tough to know what to say or do to support others in their grief. But my best advice is to be kind, compassionate and present. Care and consideration are invaluable at times like this. For many people, their companion animal is their only companion and those living alone may find it harder to recover from such an experience when their companion animal was their whole world. Service, Assistance and Emotional support animals can be prime examples of this. You can't go wrong by being genuine and telling your friend that you really are sorry for their loss.

Watching those close to us in distress can be incredibly difficult and we want to say something profound, helpful and with meaning to console them.

Sometimes we just don't know what to say and perhaps say nothing at all. In some instances, we may feel that saying nothing is better than saying the wrong thing. This doesn't mean that we don't care so be honest and tell your friend exactly that. Let them know that you care but you just don't know what to say. Sometimes a sympathetic look and a comforting touch on the arm can speak volumes and be better received than a well-meaning but insensitive remark. You could even encourage them to speak with a counsellor about how they are feeling if you are uncomfortable with them opening up to you. There is no shame in this, you maybe just don't feel equipped to deal with this. Many counsellors (including myself) offer gift vouchers, which is an excellent way to say that you care, you know they are struggling and that you want to help. The reason I wrote this book was to reach out and help people so this could be a kind and thoughtful gift to give to a friend when you are at a loss as to what to say or do to help.

Acknowledge how your friend is feeling but don't pretend to know exactly *how* they are feeling.

How to Support Others

You can't possibly know. Everyone has a different experience of grief. And that's ok. Many people view pet bereavement as an overreaction but it's important to remember that each individual is entitled to feel whatever they are feeling whether other people understand it or not; and nobody has the right to invalidate those feelings. Grief has no time limits. Never ask if they are still not over it. Just because one person reached acceptance within days or weeks, doesn't mean that everyone does. Some people can grieve for months or years. Let them know that you are ready to listen if they are ready to talk and that they are entitled to feel whatever they are feeling. However, if their demeanour causes you concern, ask them to contact their doctor or indeed do it for them. Some people have been known to feel suicidal so a call to the emergency services would not be inappropriate.

I have mentioned Disenfranchised Grief throughout this book, and it is best described as grief that is not acknowledged or accepted in society. Examples of saying the wrong thing would be 'it's just a…' or asking if they will get another one. Both of those show a complete lack of understanding and empathy so please just stay clear of such comments. 'It's just a...' is the gateway to Disenfranchised Grief. Don't be that person. It may be 'just a...' to you but that was their companion whom they adored, and such comments should be kept to yourself regardless of species. I'm sure you wouldn't want to be remembered for your insensitivity so just don't say it. They may well get another companion when they are ready, but it is not your place to make that suggestion when they are clearly still grieving. The reason for this is that many people feel that a 'replacement' for their companion animal would disrespect the bond they shared or that their pet is completely irreplaceable. It is up to your friend to broach the subject when they are in such a place to consider doing so. Telling your friend that their pet is in a better place is not helpful either as to your friend, the best place was with them. Nor is saying that everything happens for a reason when they are really struggling to make sense of the situation.

I was recently made aware of a local girl who actually lost her job because she was too grief-stricken

How to Support Others

to work her shift. She informed her employer of the death of her fourteen-year-old dog, who had been part of the family since the girl was four years old, only to be met with a lack of compassion and the threat of being fired if she did not find someone to cover her shift. Unfortunately, she was unable to work or find cover and did indeed lose her job. I am utterly appalled at the insensitivity of this employer and indeed their lack of good business sense and practice. Surely allowing her a day or two to grieve would have been more beneficial than firing her. A little compassion goes a long way to strengthening professional relationships and is certainly a lot cheaper than paying another employee overtime until a replacement is both recruited and trained to do the job which also incurs extra expense. My personal view is that it would be good practice for employers to include a reasonable policy for employees who have suffered pet bereavement. Even if it's just a day or two, it's not a big ask in the grand scheme of things but would mean a great deal to your employees, show compassion and save money. I am happy to consult on the matter and advise employers on how best to support their staff members.

Being a supportive friend isn't always easy but by giving someone the opportunity to reflect on what has happened, you're being a good friend. If you and your friends are religious, it may comfort them if you tell them that they/their family are in your prayers. If you're not religious, your thoughts will do just as well. I quite like to share my fondest memories of friend's pets. Julie's cat Angel was quite famous for photobombing and making an appearance on video calls which always caused great amusement.

Grief can be very isolating and very often people isolate themselves as they just don't feel very sociable. This can be especially true in the stage of depression. If they are not feeling like going out, offer to just sit with them. You could offer to cook them a nice meal to keep their strength up. Very often people neglect their self-care or just can't be bothered cooking while they are grieving. If they decline, don't take it personally, this isn't about you. Even if they don't feel like company right now, I'm certain they will appreciate your kindness and will let you know when they are ready. Take things in baby steps with your friend and once they are feeling a bit stronger you could suggest a spa day, movie night, sporting event or a meal out. I practice guided meditation with many of my clients so attending a group meditation might be a nice activity to do together and be of practical use to your friend without being too overwhelming because you are there with them and the aim is relaxation and mental clarity.

Whatever you decide to do to support your friend, make sure it is appropriate and personal to them. Be thoughtful and be kind. Always.

Chapter 10

Coping Mechanisms

This is the chapter that most people will be interested in and I will not be at all offended if you have jumped straight into the book here. However what I would like to stress at this point, should this be the case, is that you will not fully heal until you acknowledge your feelings and emotions of grief and allow yourself to feel whatever you are feeling so it is worthwhile reading the previous chapters so that you know what to expect and that what you are feeling is normal. However, in extremes of emotion and grief, medical intervention may be advisable and necessary. Always ask for help if you need it, there is no shame in asking for support. There is no quick fix or miracle cure for grief. If there was, somebody would have already invented it and made a fortune. Without tooting my own horn too loudly, my clients tell me that my holistic approach to counselling provides a good service by pulling together many different coping strategies as well as listening in an empathetic manner. I have taken the time to research and educate myself in various healthy practices in order to provide a better service to my clients. Some taster courses have enabled me to delve deeper into techniques which I think are extremely useful in the grieving process. Details can be found on my website and Facebook page for The Scottish Pet Bereavement Counselling Service.

There are 2 types of coping mechanisms, healthy and unhealthy. Obviously when I work with my clients, I encourage them to follow the guidance I give them on healthy coping strategies and not the unhealthy ones. You don't need to be Albert Einstein to know that 'recreational drugs' and alcohol are not a good idea, but I feel obliged to mention it anyway.

Let's explore some healthy coping mechanisms which many of my clients find helpful.

Counselling – Of course this will be top of my list as a Pet Bereavement Counsellor. At times it can be immensely helpful to speak to a trained counsellor about how we are feeling as they are skilled in empathetic listening. We often do not want to burden our friends and family with how we are feeling or perhaps we feel that they are not as sympathetic as we might hope. Disenfranchised Grief, which we have touched on throughout this book, is grief which is not acknowledged or accepted by society. These feelings of grief can very often be dismissed by those in our circle, leaving us feeling hurt and isolated in our grief. In some cases, pet bereavement has been completely trivialised or mocked which is incredibly hurtful. Please know that your feelings are your feelings, and nobody has the right to tell you that what you are feeling is wrong or silly. Engaging the services of a counsellor is a good solution to this as you are their priority and they want to listen and support you without judgement. There is great comfort to be had in knowing that someone is fully present while you are speaking and understands what a rollercoaster of emotions you are on.

Journaling – Journaling can be quite a cathartic and therapeutic experience. Journaling is not limited to keeping a diary of notable events, how you are feeling and what emotions you are experiencing but delves a little deeper and can also be writing a letter or capturing a moment through creative writing. Journaling can also take the form of a 'boast book' where my clients can write about their positive attributes, successes and achievements. We can be extremely hard on ourselves at times, so it is good to have something to refer to which reminds us of the positivity in our lives. A gratitude journal is also a good idea and we shall look at that in more detail in the section covering gratitude. Both the boast book and gratitude journal can be particularly helpful during the 'Depression' phase of grief and help build resilience.

Writing about an experience, in this case pet bereavement, helps us to put what we are feeling into words which can often be difficult. It also increases our emotional development, emotional intelligence and emotional awareness. This in turn can make us feel more empowered.

We might feel that we express our feelings quite well on a day to day basis however when an upsetting event occurs, we often keep the most painful feelings and emotions bottled up inside where they are left to fester and remain unprocessed. We can often become stuck in that place where these unprocessed emotions become more of an issue. The more we write, the better it feels to unburden ourselves which can bring clarity and understanding of the situation as we allow ourselves to open up and give an honest account of what is going on inside rather than putting a brave face on it and telling everyone that we are fine. It allows us to reflect in a positive and constructive way.

It is however worth noting, that occasionally journaling can open the floodgates and bring to the surface deep rooted trauma from the past for some people which may not have been sufficiently dealt with at the time. If that happens, it may be wise to engage the services of a healthcare professional who is qualified in that area.

Gratitude & Neuroplasticity – Research has shown that it takes approximately 21 days to form a habit. Nerve cells in the brain are also known as 'neurons'. Connections between neurons are known as 'neuro pathways'. The brain's ability to form new connections and pathways is known as **neuroplasticity.** Each neuro pathway is associated with one or more behaviours or thoughts. Each time the action is repeated the pathway is strengthened. I'm sure you can see where I am going with this.

Of course, some habits are easier to form than others. For example, if you feel like you are not drinking enough water, you can make a conscious decision to remedy this by making a point of say, drinking a pint of water every morning to increase your regular daily intake. This would be a relatively easy habit to form. A habit which can be a bit harder to commit to might be going to the gym every day. This can take a lot of effort and can sometimes take a bit longer to form as a habit. We can deliberately choose to take control of our emotional well-being in a number of ways which includes positive self-talk. If we repeatedly tell ourselves that 'today will be a good day' and start out on a positive note, chances are that our general feelings about each day will improve. However, if you start out in a negative frame of mind, it's highly likely that the day will not be so good.

Another habit which is easy to form, is gratitude. It is possible to re-write your bad day. Sometimes during the grieving process, the outlook can appear pretty bleak. It can be really difficult to see a time when you will be happy again. It is often said that practising gratitude increases our levels of happiness. Of a normal day, we will see beauty all around us but whilst in the grips of grief, it may not be so obvious, and we might have to really look for it. But trust me, it is still there. When we take a moment to look for that beauty or joy in a day, things don't seem quite so bad. We realise that we have something to be thankful for. We might appreciate a kind word from a friend or take a walk and notice a beautiful garden in our neighbourhood or simply observe a bumble bee going about it's business. If we do this on a continual basis, it will become a habit, we will see more and more, and things may not feel as negative as they once did. It can be a very comforting thing to keep a Gratitude Journal and note down things that we are thankful for on a daily basis.

In the context of pet bereavement, we can recall and be grateful for all the happy memories that we have of our companion. Special memories could be written down in your Gratitude Journal as they come to you. Fond memories of a special day out or a trip they came on or perhaps just the memory of snuggling up on a rainy afternoon or a time when they gave you comfort in their constant companionship just by being there. A time will come when you look back on these occasions with great happiness and comfort instead of sadness.

Always remember that being genuinely thankful for things, people, places or experiences releases the feel-good chemicals in the brain.

Meditation & Mindfulness – I am a huge fan of meditation. It is, in my opinion, the best way to quiet all the mind chatter and help us regain balance within ourselves. During times of grief we can struggle to cope with all the thoughts and emotions that are swirling around inside us which can leave us feeling a lot of inner turmoil, anxious and generally discombobulated. Mindfulness is a great tool to utilise to stay present and 'in the moment'. As a bit of an 'overthinker' myself, it is easy to get stuck in a circle of thought, but I find mindfulness practice extremely helpful to keep things in perspective.

Meditation has been widely recognised as hugely beneficial for hundreds of years and this is a great habit to form in general and not just to get you through this distressing time in your life. Meditation helps us to focus and lowers the levels of the stress hormone Cortisol within the body which, due to reduced levels of stress, in turn lowers the blood pressure in those experiencing high blood pressure. It's important to recognise what you need at this time.

I lead a guided meditation with my clients if they are open to trying it. The meditations I utilise are based on relaxation, self- compassion and mindfulness. Visualisation can also be helpful in addition to the use of mantras. There are many guided meditations available online or you can download apps such as Headspace or Calm to your phone.

Coping Mechanisms

Yoga – I have been practising yoga on and off since the late 1990s. Yes, THAT long! I can't speak highly enough of yoga as a form of exercise for both the body and mind. The health benefits of yoga are well documented. Not only does yoga increase your flexibility, muscle strength and tone, it also helps to strengthen your bones, improves balance, reduces excess weight, improves digestion and boost your circulation. Yoga has become increasingly popular in recent times to aide recovery from injury and is very popular with professional sportsmen and women. There are also many mental and emotional benefits to practising yoga. It increases your happiness, helps you focus and boosts your inner strength and self-esteem. It can also be a nice social activity as the yoga community is extremely welcoming, non-judgmental and has a strong focus on positivity and emotional wellbeing. There are many different types of yoga which vary in levels of simplicity or difficulty depending on what way you look at it but as you gain experience your ability to participate in more challenging practices increases. I do not claim to be an expert or a yogi, but I enjoy it and find it to be of huge personal benefit. If I may offer some motivation, B.K Iyengar who developed Iyengar Yoga (which is good for beginners) was still doing headstands in his 80s. I think it's worth doing for those bragging rights alone! I gain clarity of mind and also maintain mobility and flexibility physically. Yoga can be particularly useful in processing emotions and your instructor will inform you of the 'release' that you might feel during each particular practice as you let go of emotional tension. It is important to listen to your body and not push yourself beyond your limits. If you ever feel a little overwhelmed by emotions stirred up during your practice, it is perfectly acceptable to take a moment to yourself in child's pose.

Building Resilience – Resilience is basically one's ability to 'bounce back' from adversity. I can think of few more adverse situations than the loss of a loved one, so working on our resilience is super important before and during the grieving process. It may surprise you to learn that resilient people allow themselves time to acknowledge and process their feelings. They know that it is an important part of the healing process to let themselves feel sad, upset, lonely or whatever negative emotion they are feeling however they do not dwell for too long and are more likely to address the situation in a pro-active and positive way as they believe that they are in control of their lives rather than being at the mercy of others or external influences.

There are many things that we can do to increase our level of resilience. As previously mentioned, journaling and counselling can help us reflect on events and our emotions in less negative way. Very often this will enable us to learn and grow or perhaps even see a silver lining such as our pet being rehomed to someone with more time to spend with them or having a more suitable home environment. We might even make a list of things that we are looking forward to.

SMART Goals are often used in resilience building as well as in a professional setting. SMART Goals are Specific, Measurable, Achievable, Relevant and Timebound. It is perfectly normal to feel less sociable whilst grieving for a companion animal. We may set a SMART goal to help get ourselves back out there, take up a new hobby or exercise regime. Resilient people keep an optimistic outlook on life which helps us to feel that our goals really are achievable.

Very often when we switch on the television or log on to the internet, we are bombarded with negativity. It is completely within our power to choose to consume positive rather than negative media. I would highly recommend limiting social media intake and exposure to negativity at this time. We can instead choose to listen to an uplifting podcast or watch something joyful or inspiring with a strong feel good factor.

Healthy Eating & Living – My number one piece of advice to my clients is to avoid leaning on alcohol for support. Solace is seldom found in a bottle. In fact, more often than not it makes things worse as alcohol alters the levels of serotonin which in turn can increase feelings of anxiety and depression. Once the initial release of endorphins and dopamine wear off, we can feel depressed or indeed more depressed than we may have been in the first place. The best thing to drink is simply water; of which the recommended daily intake is 2 litres. 70% of the brain is water thus when dehydrated, the brain is less effective. Caffeine, sugary drinks and alcohol increase dehydration. Dehydration increases stress hormones/cortisol levels.

As for smoking cigarettes, short term, nicotine reduces stress levels. Long term, levels of stress increase and reduces the body's ability to produce dopamine. Research also suggests nicotine damages certain pathways in the brain that regulate mood. Find a method of cutting back and save the money for a reward.

By eating a healthy and balanced diet of fruit, vegetables, grains, sources of protein, healthy fats and dairy (or alternative dietary supplements), our bodies will absorb all the nutrients we need to support good physical, emotional and mental health which will undoubtedly improve our mood and ability to deal with setbacks. Cooking could also become a healthy habit or hobby so really, there is nothing to lose and everything to gain.

Positive Mental Health Habits – In my opinion, the distress of the grieving process is greatly eased by developing positive mental health habits. Which can simply be described as replacing our bad habits with good mental health habits. Improving your mental health is a consistent process of self-care, self-compassion and personal development. Good mental health is most definitely a benefit in the healing process of pet bereavement. It makes sense that if our mental health is in poor condition that the feelings and emotions associated with grieving will be felt more intensely and for longer.

Through counselling and journaling, we may be able to identify and therefore address many of our bad mental health habits. We can identify what we can handle on your own and what we need support with by closely examining the results of our counselling and journaling sessions.

It is important to surround ourselves with positive, encouraging, and supportive people and to nurture and maintain our personal relationships in order to develop a reliable support network. We never know when a 'wobble' day may occur without warning therefore knowing you have a circle you can depend on for support is hugely beneficial. It's better to have it and not need it than need it and not have it.

Daily exercise, even for just 30 minutes, has been proven to have a positive impact on our physical and emotional wellbeing. It also helps to build resilience. Exercise releases endorphins which make us feel good and also promotes better sleep. It is also beneficial to find a hobby that helps you decompress and relax such as hiking, jogging or cookery as previously mentioned. Taking in a good amount of fresh, clean air whilst doing so is even better.

Shut off all laptops, computers, tablets and phones at least an hour before bed and get at least 7-9 hours of quality sleep. In today's online world it is all too easy to say that we are going to bed then spend an hour scrolling through social media on our telephones. The 'blue light' which comes from our devices inhibits the body's ability to produce the sleep hormone melatonin. Grieving is absolutely exhausting physically, mentally and emotionally therefor it is essential to try and maintain a good sleeping pattern in keeping with our natural circadian rhythm which is also known as 'the body clock'.

Practice healthy and positive self-talk. At a time where everything seems terribly negative and we are full of negative emotions such as guilt and anger, it is of utmost importance to practice self-compassion and positive self-talk in order to nurture a more optimistic and positive outlook. It's not about deluding ourselves; it's about giving ourselves a kindness based honest appraisal and speaking to ourselves the way we would speak to our best friends. If a friend were feeling guilty about the death of their companion animal, there is no way you would say to them that it was all their fault and that they are a terrible person. So why would you say this to yourself?

I hope that you have found this chapter, indeed this book, informative and comforting. It has been my pleasure to share some of what I have learned with you. Please, if nothing else, know that you are not alone in this.

References

www.dictionary.com

https://www.petmd.com/cat/infographic/infographic-use-quality-life-scale-decide-when-put-your-cat-down

www.grief.com

https://vet.osu.edu/vmc/companion/our-services/honoring-bond-support-animal-owners

https://www.everydayhealth.com/news/ways-anger-ruining-your-health/#:~:text=In%20one%20study%2C%20Harvard%20University%20scientists%20found%20that,RELATED%3A%204%20Ways%20to%20Let%20Go%20of%20Anger

https://academichelp.net/samples/academics/essays/expository/why-anger-is-bad-for-your-health.html

https://newrenaissance.us/2019/10/06/anger-weakens-immune-system/

www.helpguide.org/articles/healthy-living/the-mental-health-benefits-of-exercise.htm

https://www.udemy.com/course/help-your-stress-and-depression-through-diet/

Author Bio

Wendy Andrew is a qualified Pet Bereavement Counsellor who studied with The International School for Canine Psychology and Behaviour Ltd. prior to opening The Scottish Pet Bereavement Counselling Service.

Wendy initially studied pet bereavement counselling in order to support her dog walking clients however quickly realised that this service should be available to everyone everywhere and brought the business online.

Having grown up in an agricultural area on the outskirts of Glasgow, Wendy has been a lifelong animal lover and with her parents being Kennel Club registered Labrador breeders, this really was a natural career path for her.

Wendy has been a vegetarian since the age of 14 due to her love of animals and is an advocate for animal welfare. She is committed to providing a holistic service to her counselling clients and is also a qualified meditation teacher. She has studied various practices and techniques in order to support her clients through the grieving process so that that they can heal and perhaps open their hearts and homes again one day, should they feel that is the right thing for them to do.

To find out more about Wendy's service, visit her website or social media pages.

www.thescottishpetbereavementcounsellingservice.com

www.facebook.com/thescottishpetbereavementcounsellingservice

the_spbcs

The_SPBCS

Printed in Great Britain
by Amazon